Walking Telluride

HISTORY, SIGHTS,
and STORIES

Erica Kinias

Copyright © 2015 **Durango Herald Small Press**

Published in collaboration with the Telluride Historical Museum

Erica Kinias

ISBN: 978-1-887805-39-1
Library of Congress Control Number: 2015942411

Editor: Elizabeth A. Green
Design and Layout: Lisa Snider

www.thedurangoheraldsmallpress.com

Get Ready,

You're about to go on a history scavenger hunt through a remarkable jewel in the crown of the Rocky Mountains!

Telluride is the quintessential mining boom town, and this tour will help you explore and learn a bit about the people and events that have shaped this beautiful place. For such a small town, there is a lot to see and do here.

Who knew history could be so much fun?

At each stop along the tour, a clue photo will guide you to an interesting building or landmark. Find the clue, then turn the page to see stories and photos that make Telluride's fascinating history come alive. As you follow the tour route, you'll see where immigrants settled, where businesses and warehouses were located, and where the merchants, bankers, and mine owners lived.

Your tour starts at the Rio Grande Southern Railroad Depot, toward the south end of Townsend Street. (You can take the free bus from the Visitors Center or use metered parking on adjacent streets.) You'll walk through a residential area, the notorious red-light district, and

FYI:

There's always something under construction in Telluride, so be prepared for small detours.

The houses on this tour are privately owned; please view them from the sidewalk.

on to our main commercial street. Then you'll stroll along the beautiful north side residential district of town and finish at the Telluride Historical Museum.

The full tour is about 1½ miles, and most complete it in 1½ to 2 hours. The tour can be divided into segments to accommodate time restrictions or interests. The map on the back cover will keep you on track and on sidewalks the whole way.

Just a note

This is a mountain town, so there are some hills along the way. Just take it easy and enjoy the scenery. Be aware of the altitude – 8,750 feet above sea level – and stop to rest if necessary.

Take your camera and stop for water or refreshments along the way. Enjoy!

KEY:

 You found it!

Boldface type in the text identifies people or places in photographs.

Telluride's significance in American history was recognized in 1961 when Congress designated it as a National Historic Landmark District, in recognition of the way our architecture preserves the legacy of the American West's mining era. The designation includes 300 historic buildings deemed as contributing to its architectural heritage. It is one of only 2,500 such landmark districts nationwide. Included in the designation are several residential neighborhoods, a red-light district, and Lone Tree Cemetery. Numerous late Victorian era and vernacular buildings also are listed individually on the National Register of Historic Places.

🏠 Contributor to Historic District

🔍 Items that can be seen in the
Telluride Historical Museum at the end of the tour.

Get Set,

The long valley and soaring 14,000-foot peaks that surround it were the Ute Indians' sacred hunting grounds for centuries. Prospectors arrived in the early 1870s, looking for gold nuggets or flakes in the streams. Soon, men were scouring the mountains for veins of gold and silver. The first placer claim was filed in August 1875, and only a few months later the first mining claim was filed. Those initial mines proved incredibly rich and attracted a flood of fortune seekers.

In the beginning, most people lived and conducted business in tents or log cabins. The first settlement, San Miguel City, was overshadowed within a few years by a fast-developing town farther east into the box canyon. Originally called Columbia but soon renamed Telluride, the upstart town became the county seat in 1883.

In 1884, a freighter spent $30,000 to clear a road from the north, so he could haul food and supplies to Telluride. But the town's turning point came in the 1890s with the arrival of the Rio Grande Southern Railroad and cheap, reliable alternating current electricity. In fact, just a few miles outside of town, the world's first production and transmission of AC power for commercial purposes took place. This important milestone forever altered Telluride's fortunes as well as the daily life of its residents.

A railroad connection also was pivotal, not only for transporting mining supplies and ore, but also for bringing large quantities of supplies to build Telluride's beautiful homes and elaborate commercial buildings. Many of the town's first structures were replaced by larger, more permanent, and stylish buildings as the population grew from 766 in 1890 to a peak of 5,000 in 1908.

The young town had its troubles. Labor strife at the turn of the twentieth century led to violent strikes, and an influenza epidemic devastated the town in 1918. By 1929, mining was all but over, except for a resurgence of base metals mining in the 1940s. The last mine closed in 1978.

Yet Telluride has proven its resilience time and again. Even in tough times, this town has known how to throw a good party, whether it is a riotous competition or an elaborate Fourth of July parade.

Just as the population declined and businesses closed in the 1960s, creative, free-spirited people were drawn to Telluride's beautiful natural surroundings, and its isolation. The area's potential as the world's next winter sports Mecca drew attention as well.

Today, with its blend of history and contemporary culture, Telluride is one community that enthusiastically looks toward its future while never losing sight of its past.

... Go!

Find this window
on the building in front of you.

 Like passengers arriving in Telluride at the turn of the nineteenth century, you're starting your tour from the depot.

THE TRAIN DEPOT 🏠

The depot's arched brackets were a standard feature of all **Rio Grande Southern depots,** as was the building's color scheme. After railroad service ceased, the depot stood empty and neglected for many years. Thanks to the careful matching of original paint chips by a dedicated restoration team, the building's original color scheme has been restored.

PATHFINDERS

Telluride might have quietly faded away after the initial discovery of gold, its mineral riches too difficult to extricate from the mountains and too costly to ship to smelters, if it weren't for freighter **Dave Wood**, who spent a fortune clearing a road through heavily timbered mountains to haul food, machinery, dynamite, coal, and more to the booming mining town, and Otto Mears, who became known as the Pathfinder of the San Juans.

RAILS TO TELLURIDE

In late 1889, **Otto Mears** created the Rio Grande Southern Railroad with a group of prominent citizens, including the state governor, and set his sights on it reaching Telluride.

To finance the venture, Mears sold more than $9 million in stocks and bonds.

When the first Rio Grande Southern Railroad engine chugged into this depot on November 23, 1890, it had an immeasurable impact on the future growth of Telluride. The railroad not only brought far greater quantities of essential goods into town, but also transported rich ores faster, in greater quantity, and farther than ever before.

Turn right and go around the depot on the porch.
Look for this railroad sign on the back.

This signal was for trains on the tracks, which were below the porch, next to the river.

IT WAS RUMORED

Brothers Lon and William Remine came to the San Juan Mountains in the 1870s and befriended the powerful **Utes**, who told them of early Spanish mining activity along the river. Their placer claim – the first in the area – fueled rumors of Spanish treasure and lost mines. By 1875, hundreds of men were working the gravel along the San Miguel. Few of them thought about their impact on the Indians' traditional hunting and fishing grounds.

ALL THAT GLITTERS

While placer mining on the San Miguel did not prove very profitable, **prospectors** who came to the valley attracted larger mining outfits and investors. Decades after his arrival here, Lon Remine told a Telluride local that in those first years of placer mining on the San Miguel River, he made at least $15 a day.

STAKING A CLAIM

In 1875, a year after the federal Hayden Survey mapped the San Juans, prospector John Fallon scaled a craggy, 13,000-foot granite barrier to reach Marshall Basin. Rather than panning for nuggets, he was looking for the mother lode. He staked five claims on an enormously rich gold vein. His first ore shipment alone put a $10,000 profit in his pockets. Fallon's Sheridan Group mines yielded almost $20 million before the end of the century. In 1899, Fallon sold half-interest in the mines for $15 million dollars.

Great lodes, like the Sheridan, Smuggler-Union, Liberty Bell, Tomboy, and Gold King, enhanced Telluride's reputation. While miners tunneled shafts into the ore-rich basins, **hydraulic mining** – blasting the earth with water – carved up the banks of the San Miguel River below with less success.

SUCCESS AT LAST

Lucien Lucius (L.L.) Nunn arrived in Telluride in 1881, after having abandoned law studies and failed as a restaurateur. By 1890, he held a large interest in the **Gold King Mine** south of Telluride, but scarce firewood and expensive coal were driving up the cost of operating mining equipment and eroding mine profits. Using an innovative Westinghouse single-phase generator – the largest then manufactured – Nunn erected a high-voltage alternating current generating station in Ames, south of Telluride. In 1891 – soon after the railroad reached Telluride – Nunn threw the switch on the world's first commercial hydroelectric AC power system. A brilliant electrical arc shot six feet into the air, and the generator hummed with electricity, revolutionizing the profitability of hardrock mining in the San Juans.

THEN THERE IS LIGHT

Electricity from the Ames Power Plant was so plentiful – and profitable – that Nunn erected five miles of power lines from the plant to town, providing street lighting for Telluride more than three decades earlier than many Eastern cities. In 1894, a Telluride Board of Trade pamphlet read, "Telluride is the most brilliantly lighted town, perhaps, in the world [thanks to] five arc lights of 1,500 candle power on Colorado Avenue."

Sixteen years later, a groundbreaking hydro-electrical plant was constructed to supply electricity to another mining operation, the Smuggler-Union. Perched at the top of its namesake 365-foot waterfall, the Bridal Veil Powerhouse included a generator and transformer plant as well as a private residence. The house and plant were added to the National Register of Historic Places in 1979 and restored in 1991. This important landmark still generates electricity for the town of Telluride.

CURRENT WARS

Nunn's gamble at Ames came at the height of the "current wars" between Westinghouse and Thomas Edison over whether alternating current (AC) or direct current (DC) electric power would prevail as an economically viable energy source. The generator at Ames proved to be extremely effective, transmitting AC electrical power two miles at a loss of less than 5 percent. Its success led to adoption of AC at much larger plants, including Niagara Falls in 1895, and its eventual dominance worldwide.

MINING LIFE

The Tomboy was Telluride's largest mine, claimed in 1886 by Otis "Tomboy" Thomas. In 1896 it produced $800,000 worth of ore and a year later more than $1.8 million. At one time, 200 to 300 men worked in the mining complex, located in Savage Basin at 11,465 feet elevation. The complex included a boarding house, schoolhouse, tennis courts, and even a bowling alley. Still, life in the mining camps was not easy. Ogda Matson Walter, a former resident at the Tomboy Mine, said the snow never fell, but raged in a horizontal flurry. Many miners of Scandinavian descent were adept skiers and it was not uncommon for them to strap on wooden skis in order to move about the basin.

3

Double back on the porch to where you started,
then walk one short block up the street to Pacific Avenue and turn
right. Watch for this bell as you walk to the middle of the block.

 You have found Finn Hall.

SOCIAL CENTER

Built in 1899, **Finn Hall** was a gathering place for Finnish families, similar to Swede-Finn Hall nearby. Finns, Swedes, and Swede-Finns were distinct, often separate groups, each using their own language and customs. This hall's open design was ideal for parties, theatrical performances and holiday celebrations. Now a private residence, this front-gable building still has its large stage and painted stage curtains.

DIVERSE NEIGHBORHOOD

In Telluride's early years, Pacific Avenue was a vibrant home to hundreds who worked in the mines or local businesses, including **immigrants** from Finland, Sweden, Switzerland, Germany, Austria, Italy, France, England, and Scotland. Finns had their own grocery store, boarding houses, public saunas, and social hall. By 1900, more than 100 people

from Finland called Telluride home. Though proud Americans, they maintained strong emotional and social ties to their native country.

" At Christmastime, the tree in the hall went from floor to ceiling. Everyone brought their gifts, even for people within their own family, and put them under the tree. The Finnish kids would get on stage and recite little pieces in Finnish, and coffee and cake were served. Since the hall was heated with a potbelly stove, **Santa** simply strolled through the door at ten o'clock."

– Walter Pera

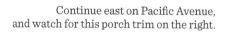
Continue east on Pacific Avenue,
and watch for this porch trim on the right.

 You have found one of many Finnish businesses.

ROOM & BOARD

Finn Town Flats was a boarding house for miners, comparable in size to many boarding houses in Telluride. Usually run by widows, boarding houses played an important part in the success of Telluride's mining industry by providing homes for men without families. The rent typically included meals and laundry service. Buildings such as the Finn Town Flats were built by hand using volunteer labor.

IN A DAY'S WORK

In the 1880s, hard-rock miners worked ten-hour shifts through every season of the year, day and night for $3 a day – minus $1 for those who boarded at the mine. Surface laborers earned even less, up to $2.50 a day. Working conditions were extremely hazardous within – and outside of – the mines. Avalanches were common in the winter and spring, often claiming lives and destroying boarding houses, tram towers, homes, railroad tracks, and trestles.

> ❝ I got out of high school when I was sixteen and went to work [at Tomboy]. I rode trip on the big **ore cart** for Babe Schuler. Babe was the motorman, and I was his tail-end rider. In and out, we made eleven trips a day – from inside the mine to the mill. I got four dollars [a day] and Babe got five. One dollar, at 15¢ a day [went] for board and room. That came out of your check. I was pretty handy at setting pins at the bowling alley. I did that for a long time. The guys wanted to bowl: 'Come on, Harry, and set the pins for us!'"
>
> – Harry Wright

Continue walking east to Oak Street
and look up at the walls of the box canyon to the east.

INGRAM FALLS TELLURIDE COLO.

 You have found Ingram Falls, one of two iconic waterfalls visible from town.

FORTUNE AT STAKE

Being a stickler for details made J.B. Ingram a very wealthy man. When John Fallon filed his Sheridan Group claims in 1875, he exceeded the maximum length. Ingram measured the claims, found the discrepancy, and pounded his own stakes on the overage. In keeping with the stealth nature of his claim, Ingram named his mine the **Smuggler**.

Although the waterfall plummets from his namesake basin, Ingram's mine is actually to the northwest, in Marshall Basin, just one mile below the Tomboy Mine. The mill for his mine was below Ingram Falls. You can see what remains of the Pandora Mill complex by following Colorado Avenue east toward the waterfall.

GREAT DAY HIKE

Ingram Falls was named after J.B. Ingram, whose nearby mine claim became Telluride's most lucrative, producing ore worth $1 million in 1899. Ingram Falls drops out of Ingram Basin more than 2,000 feet above the town and falls about 280 feet in three steps – the largest being a prominent 175-foot plunge. Today the waterfall is a popular hiking destination.

HARD ROCK MINING

Mines, mills, and the businesses that catered to them were at the heart of Telluride's economy. Mines yielded lead, zinc, copper, silver, and – most coveted of all – gold. The rock was broken in the mines high above town, and then brought by long aerial trams and pack trains down to the mills below, where it was crushed and refined. The refined ore was then shipped by railroad to smelters in Durango and beyond.

DISASTER STRIKES

On February 28, 1902, a massive **snowslide** came hurtling down Cornet Creek just northwest of Telluride, taking the Liberty Bell Mine's boarding house and some nearby bunkhouses with it. As rescue teams frantically searched for survivors, another snowslide ran, killing two of the rescuers. Then a third slide fell, sweeping away the next rescue team. By the end of the day, sixteen men were dead and ten injured. Some of the bodies were not recovered until the following spring.

👉 **Before you continue on, look north up Oak Street and see if you can spot this house.**

DAHL HOUSE

Independently run boarding houses were familiar establishments in mining boom towns like Telluride. Catering to single men and even women, boarding houses provided a room, meals, and even laundry services for lodgers.

Just to your left up Oak Street is one of Telluride's most notable boarding houses, built in 1890. By 1902 it had become the **Dahl Rooming House**, operated by **Lena Dahl** and her husband Joseph. The Dahls were Finnish immigrants who met and married in Telluride in 1897. Joseph, born 1861, had been in America since 1882. Lena, born in 1870, had arrived shortly before their marriage. The couple did not have children.

Continue east on Pacific Avenue and stop at the corner of Fir Street.
Find this stone archway across the street.

You're now facing the impressive Telluride Transfer building, built in 1889.

TRANSPORTATION HUB

In its early days, **Telluride Transfer** kept horses for the miners to ride from town to the mines. The streets of Telluride were constantly alive with the sound of horse and mule hooves as men moved to and from town and the mines. Once miners arrived at work, they often set the animals loose, letting them dash back to the Transfer by themselves, giving mothers yet another reason to admonish their children not to play in the streets.

OFF TO SCHOOL

The Transfer also operated the town's school bus. The horse-pulled wagon was affectionately called the **Monkey Cage**.

RUINS NO MORE

The Transfer's generally unremarkable masonry construction, graced only by keystone arches over windows and entrance, was typical of utilitarian buildings in Telluride's early days. As automobiles replaced horses, the building evolved into a **garage and gas station.** The roof collapsed in the 1970s, but efforts are currently underway to restore and renovate this important structure.

Turn right on Fir Street and walk a half block.
Look for your clue on the right.

You have found the Stronghouse Building in the heart of Telluride's warehouse district.

PACK STRINGS

Freighters were often justifiably described as the lifelines of the mines. Hardy teams of **mules and horses** hauled cables, machinery, supplies, and ore up and down narrow, steep trails at dizzying heights.

Aerial tramways, or "trams," were an equally vital means of transport. These marvels of engineering raised and lowered men, supplies, and ore between the mines and mills, and to transportation below. You can see replicas of these tram towers and artifacts at the Telluride Historical Museum's outdoor mining exhibit.

ANY ROCK WILL DO

The warehouse district was a busy and extremely noisy place during the 1900s. Appearance was secondary to function in this long-gabled warehouse known as the **Stronghouse Building**, built with a technique known as rubble construction. Masons used whatever rocks they could find with little concern for the finished appearance, binding them together with thick layers of mortar. Supplies were transferred between wagons, which were at the east side loading dock, and trains, which were on the south side.

LOAD 'EM OUT

Passengers arriving in Telluride disembarked at the depot on the west side of town. The trains then moved ahead to the **warehouse district** and unloaded goods here,

where they could be stored to await distribution throughout town and to the surrounding mining camps.

❝Dad helped them to rebuild the aerial tramway in 1936 from what's known as the New Mill to Pandora. He also worked on the Bullion Tram and the Pennsylvania Tram. I worked on that tramway... starting there when I was fourteen. All the men were in the army. It was 1942, so they needed help pretty bad. We built the foundations for all the towers. We used a lot of three-by-twelves, and they were all green – just hauled up from the sawmill.... I worked out there for twenty-two years."

– Malcolm "Mouse" McDonald

NO-COST LIFT

No miner could have predicted these aerial tramways would evolve into a vital part of the ski industry decades later. After the end of the tour, take a trip on the **free gondola**, which connects the town of Telluride with the town of Mountain Village and the Telluride Ski Resort. The gondola station is located on San Juan Avenue and Oak Street. This unique municipal transport system, which serves 2.5 million people a year, has an elaborate lightning protection system. After you finish your tour, you can walk from the museum down Fir Street to San Juan Avenue and turn right to reach the gondola station.

☞ As you continue toward your next stop,
you'll pass the old Telluride Ice House, now LaMarmotte.
Ice was cut from beaver ponds in the winter, then stored in
sawdust here for use through the summer.

8

Walk to the corner and turn left (east) onto West San Juan Avenue and continue for one block. Turn left again at South Pine Street. Look for your clue on the right side of the street.

 You have found one of Telluride's many houses of ill repute.

RED-LIGHT DISTRICT

Welcome to Telluride's red-light district. This is one of the oldest surviving bordellos in Telluride. The infamous **Pick & Gad** took its name from the mining tools of the time. "Gad" is a Cornish term for a pointed metal crowbar used to loosen ore. The Pick & Gad's reputation as one of the classier bordello/gambling houses made it an extremely successful establishment. Notice the stone foundation and high-quality, creamy-red brick used for the front. With its brick, columns, and molding, this building was more impressive than most houses of ill repute. Although said to be more "lady-like", the women here were no more modest than their less fortunate sisters in the trade.

LADIES OF THE EVENING

Telluride's red-light district had it all for lonely men in need of female companionship. Some sporting women offered brief episodes of companionship in cribs, usually single rooms or small houses. Some were in brothels, usually **saloons,** where the "entertainment" included liquor, gambling, and dancing. Men who could afford it frequented more opulent bordellos for their discreet encounters.

TUNEFUL SLOTS

In addition to being a bordello and music hall, the Pick & Gad cleaned out patrons' pockets with gaming machines. The Chicago-based Mills Company started producing Dewey upright models – complete with a music box on the inside – in 1899. One of these **Dewey slot machines** from the Pick & Gad survives and can be seen at the Telluride Historical Museum.

Continue to the corner and turn right on Pacific Avenue.
Look for this house detail across the street.

 The buildings you are looking at are cribs.

....

SOILED DOVES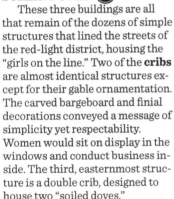

These three buildings are all that remain of the dozens of simple structures that lined the streets of the red-light district, housing the "girls on the line." Two of the **cribs** are almost identical structures except for their gable ornamentation. The carved bargeboard and finial decorations conveyed a message of simplicity yet respectability. Women would sit on display in the windows and conduct business inside. The third, easternmost structure is a double crib, designed to house two "soiled doves."

ON THE MOVE

Few cribs have survived in mining towns. Relatively transportable, the cribs were often relocated from one site to another within the town, and were often the first structures to be demolished as communities became more established. In 1979, the National Trust for Historic Preservation purchased the three **remaining cribs** as well as the Silver Bell, for $80,940. The town then purchased the properties from the Trust for $70,000, with the Trust's stipulation that the cribs be restored and used as low- to moderate-income housing. The buildings remain "contributing structures" to the town's status as a National Historic Landmark District.

> "The Pick & Gad was the big one. Then there was the Silver Bell. [My wife] Francis knew the girls well. She was working at the store, Pekkarine's. They would buy a lot of clothes from her.... One thing they did, too, if they knew you and saw you in the street, they didn't speak to you. They didn't make out so other people would know that you knew her."
> – Don O'Rourke

10

Continue on Pacific Avenue for one-half block.
Look across the street for this metal sign.

 This is Popcorn Alley.

....

NOISY DOORS

Was it the children selling popcorn here or the doors popping open and closed all hours of the day and night that gave this block its name? In its 1920s heyday, the red-light district has up to three dozen cribs and the streets were littered with popcorn. Whatever the inspiration for the name, the owner of the adjacent former crib erected this sign in 1983, long after the district had gone out of the "business."

TRUE LOVE

James Shane arrived in Telluride in 1893, hoping to secure a grubstake (a loan against prospecting profits). No one would lend to him so Jim played the piano in red-light district parlor houses and saloons.

Word spread amongst the women that he was also an artist. One prostitute, **Audrey Ford**, proposed an attractive business deal. If Shane would paint a portrait of her, he could sell it to a local establishment, earning enough money for prospecting. In return, the portrait would advertise Audrey's services.

As she posed and he painted, Audrey and Jim fell in love. He sold the painting, struck gold, and married Audrey. With a successful business of buying and selling profitable claims, they built a respectable life together. Audrey's iconic portrait hangs in the Telluride Historical Museum.

32 |

" They were not 'ladies of the night' in a bad way; they were very nice ladies. If you wanted to sell tickets – we'd have something like a St. Patrick's dance or something – you'd always ask them and they bought them. They'd tear them up and not go, of course. They just bought them as a donation."

– Elvira (Visintin) Wunderlich

FEW OPTIONS

Women who worked as **prostitutes** came from across the country – only sometimes willingly – to provide services to the many prospectors and miners. They occupied multiple social strata in the gambling and prostitution world as well as town society, although most were heavily restricted in the company they could keep and when they could be seen in town. Prostitutes rarely left the confines of the red-light district, but local merchants would stop by each establishment in the afternoons to sell the women clothes and supplies. Alcohol and drug abuse were common.

☞ **Continue on Pacific and stop at the corner.**

GOOD MONEY 🏠

As you continue on, watch for a blue, single-story building across the street. Known as the **Good Times Society**, this is an example of the range of building quality among bordellos. Although they were known euphemistically as female boarding houses, the residents earned money by entertaining men in their rooms for as much as $4 per client – more than a full day's pay for most miners. With its board and batten siding, this building's exterior looks more like an ordinary family home than the thriving house of prostitution it was.

11

Cross Spruce Street,
then turn left and walk one-half block, looking for this iron gate.

HOOSEGOW

Walk into the courtyard to view the iron jail cell, which was moved here from a mining camp high in the mountains. It is believed to have been outdoors in the camp, serving as a temporary holding cell until troublemakers could be moved into town. This **stone jail**, just beyond the courtyard, was built in 1903, by Billy Anderson, a bricklayer who owned a livery stable. It replaced a sturdy but small stacked-wood jail known as the Calaboose, which caught fire from a woodstove.

You have found Telluride's second jail.

Law enforcement in Telluride around the turn of the nineteenth century was rudimentary. Vigilante justice often prevailed, and local citizens occasionally formed posses to capture and turn in troublemakers. The most common crimes that landed men in jail were disorderly conduct, theft, assault, and, occasionally, murder.

COLORFUL LAWMAN

One of Telluride's most notorious lawmen served as marshal in the 1970s, while this small town was being transformed into a destination ski resort. **Everett Morrow** ruled with Old West bravado, and was never seen without his iconic cowboy hat and low-slung revolver. He was determined to keep the town free of drugs and misbehaving "hippies," despite the influx of newcomers.

Morrow, who was once sued for denying civil liberties, is remembered for his unconventional tactics. In one sting operation, he sent an underage buyer to visit local bars and in one night cited and closed nearly every bar in town.

Morrow left his post as marshal in his inimitable cowboy style after a newly elected town council filled with newcomers fired him. He threw his badge across the chamber floor toward the council and exclaimed, "The badge is yours, but the gun is mine."

JUSTICE AND JAIL

In April 1897, Robert Green was arrested for cutting off Louis Toy's queue – a traditional long braid of hair. When his trial was postponed indefinitely, Chinese residents in town pushed for Green to be prosecuted to the fullest extent. The newspaper warned that failure to prosecute him might "result in serious international difficulties."

A few months later, two men were arrested for fighting. They pled guilty and were fined $12.50 each. Neither man could pay, so they were sentenced to twenty days in jail.

TELLURIDE SOCIETY

In 1891, a Boston woman inquired about the town's "society" before deciding to move here. The poorly written answer she received convinced her to look elsewhere:

". . . As for society it is bang up. This is a mighty morel town, considern' that theres 69 saloons and two newspapers to a population of 1,247. But every saloon has a sine up sayin, 'All fighting must be done outside. No kilin in this room.' One two men has been killed since Monday, and tomorrow will be Wednesday. Cheatin' at gamlin is punished by linchin, and every effort is being made to put the town on a morel basis equal to Rico."

12

Walk past the old jail and cross the alley, then look across Spruce Street for your next clue.

FAVORITE BORDELLO

This building was converted from a conventional boarding house for traveling entertainers to a brothel known as the **Senate**. Of all the bordellos and the twenty-six saloons in town with more than 100 women working the line, no place was more popular than the Senate, run by Telluride's infamous madam, Betty Wagner, otherwise known as "Big Billy."

This "Senate" had nothing to do with passing laws.

SOFT HEART

"Big Billy," Betty Wagner was born in Texas in 1896. In addition to the Senate, she managed the Silver Bell and the Smuggler Inn on Colorado Avenue and rented upstairs rooms at the inn to single miners. Betty later owned and operated the Corner Café, on the corner of Spruce and Colorado Avenue. Her granddaughter, Gwen Young Carrall, recalls helping her hardworking grandmother by serving customers at the soda foundation. Betty had a tough attitude and quick temper, but was kind toward strangers and well-respected in town.

CITIES IN THE SKY

Many miners lived in company-owned boarding houses high up in the mountains. The Smuggler and **Tomboy** mines boarding houses were famous for being very spacious "small cities in the sky." The food was typically good – mining companies knew that good food helped reduce turnover rates. But when the men received their weekly or monthly salaries, they often came down into town and spent their earnings on a good meal, a bath, a visit to a saloon, and female companionship.

Continue north on Spruce Street to Colorado Avenue.
Look up to your right to find this sign.

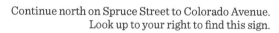

GRAND DESIGN

The **Masonic Temple** is a fantastic example of Telluride's commercial architecture. Large display windows and the double storefront entrance define the bottom level of the building as a place for business. Kickplates at the base of the windowed walls were applied for ornamentation and protection from horses' hooves and people's feet. On the second floor, the Italianate rounded arches and keystones above the tall, triple-sash windows lend an air of grandeur and permanence. The historic hanging sign displays Masonic organization symbols from top to bottom: Eastern Star, Knights Templar, Masons, and Shriners. The building has been the

You are looking at the Masonic Building on Telluride's main street.

backdrop to many Fourth of July events, including epic **Tug of War** competitions.

GALA OPENING

In 1895, **Masonic Lodge No. 56** paid $2,200 for the two lots on which to build their temple, and appointed a committee to oversee construction. Four years later, in May 1899, they celebrated completion of the temple with a gala that was attended by Grand Lodge officers from throughout Colorado. The lodge paid off all debts on the building by 1915.

CLUBS GALORE

Organizations and societies like the Masons were popular in most mining towns in the West. They offered entertainment, education, social prestige, and political unity, as well as a sense of belonging for people who were far from home and relatives. Practical benefits included burial insurance and assistance to widows and children when married miners were disabled or killed. Local chapters of national organizations in Telluride included Woodmen of the World, Elks, Freemasons, Fraternal Order of the Eagles, **Knights Templar**, Knights of Pythias, Independent Order of Odd Fellows, Knights of the Maccabees, Foresters of America, and Veterans of Foreign Wars. Women's organizations included the Rebekah Lodge, Women of Woodcraft, Order of the Eastern Star, Ladies of the Maccabees, and Commonweal Club. By 1905, there were more than twenty active clubs in Telluride, including at least one children's organization, the Boy Scouts.

BUSY WOMAN

One woman, Henrietta Glenn, kept very busy with such groups in Telluride. She held offices in at least five organizations, including the Rebekahs, Eastern Star, Ladies of Maccabees, **Degree of Pocahontas**, and the Altar Society of St. Patrick's Church. In 1911, Henrietta was appointed registrar for the Colorado State Board of Health, with responsibility for recording all births and deaths in the Telluride area. Her husband, Ivy L. Glenn, was an undertaker, assayer, furniture store owner, and sometime miner, and also served as coroner. The couple's house at 120 North Willow Street still bears their name, even though they moved to Pueblo in 1913.

Cross Colorado Avenue and find this decorative detail
on a building in front of you.

 You have found the oldest surviving commercial building in Telluride.

CLASSIC STOREFRONT

Probably built before 1886, the **Sheridan Pool Hall,** has a false front, which was typical of storefronts in Western mining towns. The square façade and wood cornice make the building appear large and formal. In 1893, Englishman Samuel Peters and a partner owned the pool hall. Peters came to Telluride in the mid-1880s. His wife and children did not adapt to life in the mountains, so the family returned to England in 1896. A year later, Peters came back to Telluride, leaving his family behind. He died in 1897, at the age of 39, without ever seeing them again.

HIGH-STEPPING

By the mid-1880s, wooden buildings were replacing **crude log cabins** and tents as money flowed into Telluride from distant investors. But those increasingly grand buildings faced a mud street filled with animal waste, so a substantial network of elevated boardwalks was installed to keep pedestrians out of the muck.

GOLD VS. SILVER

The 1890 Sherman Silver Purchase Act directed the federal government to buy millions of ounces of silver, making the U.S. the world's second-largest buyer of silver and helping mining communities in the San Juans thrive.

By 1893, with the country facing its worst economic depression, President Cleveland claimed federal gold reserves were being drained. The act was repealed, creating a rift between gold standard supporters in the East and silver supporters in the West and South. Colorado's silver-rich mining communities were economically crippled. Telluride was fortunate because many of its mines yielded more gold than silver, so the impact was minimal here. Between January 1895 and November 1896, the Tomboy Mine alone generated $625,000 in gold mining profits.

15

Walk west on Colorado Avenue
and look for this clue on your right.

Great job! You have found the historic Roma Bar.

....

A SURVIVOR

In contrast to the Masonic Temple, the **Roma Bar's** simple, utilitarian architecture suggests that this building was not designed to be permanent when it was built in 1885. In its early years, it served as a warehouse, restaurant, and grocery before becoming the Roma Bar and Café after prohibition ended. A fire in 1973 destroyed the adjacent building, but the bar survived. The Roma was rebuilt in the early 1980s.

GOLD THIEVES

In the early 1900s, the bar was known as a place to process "high-grade" gold that had been taken illegally from the mines. Miners would conceal pieces of gold-bearing ore in their clothing or lunch buckets, then bring them to such **illicit operations.** In a 1940 bust, federal officers found a small ball mill, a crusher, and other gold-processing equipment in the basement.

LEGALLY DRY

In December 1913, more than three years before national **prohibition**, Colorado became legally dry. It did not take long for a few individuals in Telluride to start bootlegging for profit. Despite all the laws and ordinances forbidding the production or sale of hard liquor, it flowed freely in several back rooms. Most townspeople simply looked the other direction. "Prohibition was stupid anyway," one old-timer rationalized. Twenty years later in 1933, Coloradans agreed and voted to ratify the twenty-first Amendment to the United States Constitution, which repealed prohibition.

66 There were stills all around town. ...They had spotters stationed down at Placerville. When the train stopped to unload baggage, the Denver train – that would be the one from the north – they would come on that train, the 'Prohibs,' we called them. By the time they got to Telluride, a phone call would warn everyone to ditch the still and get rid of the liquor. And when they'd finally arrive, they wouldn't find anything. "

– Walter "Shorty" Larson

SODA, ANYONE?

In the 1920s, the Telluride Town Council granted dozens of **soft-drink parlor** licenses to restaurants and hotels, including such former saloons as the Senate, Pick & Gad, and Roma Bar. In 1924, the owner of the Roma Bar, Carlo Girardi, received his soft-drink parlor license. Six months later, federal agents fanned out over Telluride's business district, searching every parlor. Officers arrested Girardi after agents claimed they found 800 gallons of wine at the Roma. By  mid-1925, parlors that were temporarily closed for possession of alcohol or the presence of stills, were quickly back in business.

16

Walk west on Colorado Avenue
and look for this clue on your right.

 Check out what's in the Free Box, before continuing on the tour.

....

ECCENTRIC ICON

The **1970s** breathed a whole new life into the sleepy mountain town of Telluride. People looking for an escape from modern life or attracted to the grandeur of the mountain peaks, brought new ideas to town. In those days Telluride was cheaper and more eccentric, and the **Free Box** became a local icon. People hew strictly to the Free Box credo: Take something, leave something. Over the years, a range of items have been donated, from designer clothing to computers and cell phones. Telluride's Free Box has come to represent a new generation of residents – ski bums, second-home owners, and everyone in between.

BRINGING IN A NEW ERA

It was not the 1970s newcomers who spearheaded Telluride's economic boom. Local residents, miners, and shopkeepers – including Billy "Senior" Mahoney, Donald O'Rourke, Chic Carriere, and Robert "Bucky" Schuler – had long cherished the idea that a ski area would be the next best thing for the mountain community. Visionary businessman and lawyer **Joseph Zoline** made the initial purchase of land and hired Mahoney as the ski company's first mountain manager and site consultant, thus sealing Telluride's future in "white gold." The Telluride Ski Company officially opened in 1972. In its first season, 30,000 people skied the mountain. A one-day lift ticket was $7.50 and a season pass was $175.

> 🖝 **After scoping out the Free Box,**
> **look diagonally across Colorado Avenue.**

AMBITIOUS BUILDING 🏠

The **Nunn and Wrench Building** – an addition to the front of an original 1890 stone structure – was built in 1899 by San Miguel Bank and Gold King Mine owner L.L. Nunn and A.M. Wrench, another prominent businessman. The structure was to be 100 feet long and 120 feet deep, with a basement under half of it. With its long, low profile, the single-story building appears weighed down by its flat roof and ornate metal cornice. The building is part of the largest commercial block in Telluride's downtown district.

Space was rented for clothing, plumbing, and hardware stores before it was even completed. Over the years, it has housed a livery stable, saloons, a department store, and a post office. Maps from the prohibition era indicate the building was occupied by "soda shops" – conveniently located near the "female boarding houses."

WIDE STREET

You may have noticed that Colorado Avenue seems exceptionally wide for a mountain town. Pack trains, sometimes in excess of thirty mules or horses, would often assemble and have to turn around on this street as they were loaded with supplies for the mines, including cables for the tramways that crisscrossed between mines and mills. Before the train arrived in 1890, the street would be filled with freight wagons that were laden with supplies and pulled by teams of oxen or horses. In more recent years, the width has made Colorado Avenue an ideal venue for **parades** and concerts.

17

Continue walking west on Colorado Avenue
and look for this clue in the middle of the block.

 This is the Bank of Telluride building.

FOREIGN MONEY

With two grand columns flanking the entry, Greek revival influences of the grey brick **Bank of Telluride** building set it apart from other commercial structures along Colorado Avenue. Money from Eastern and foreign investors poured into Telluride in the early years as one mining claim after another assayed out at unparalleled values. Built in 1890, the Bank of Telluride thrived during Telluride's boom years and weathered some tough times as well.

DESPERATE TIMES

High-grading, which had always gone on to some degree, drew particular law enforcement attention in the waning years of the Great Depression. Before the Roma Bar bust, Sheriff Lawrence Warrick arrested a ring of Telluride miners who had smuggled rich pieces of ore out of the mines. The *Denver Post* reported the theft of "$50,000 to $100,000 worth of gold" from the Smuggler-Union and the Tomboy, making it the "largest high-grading case in the state's history."

SCANDAL

When the stock market collapsed in 1929, scores of mines closed and Telluride's population plummeted to less than 600. To prevent a rush of creditors,

the bank temporarily closed. Hardworking Telluride residents were about to lose their life savings.

The colorful, high-profile president, **Charles "Buck" Waggoner**, concocted a complicated financial scheme to defraud some large New York financial institutions by having them transfer money to the bank. Some historians disagree on his motives, but whatever his intentions, Waggoner ended up in jail and the Bank of Telluride folded in 1929. It would not reopen for thirty years.

In February 1939, Waggoner told a newspaper reporter he had known what he was doing and accepted full blame.

Continue west on Colorado Avenue.
Find the Mahr Building on the right and look down for this clue.

You have found a storefront that arrived by train.

IRON STOREFRONT

The **Mahr Building** was built in 1892, on the site of the former San Miguel Valley Bank, using an 1887 façade manufactured by the Mesker Brothers Foundry in St. Louis, Missouri. Such iron storefronts couldn't be delivered to Telluride until the train arrived in 1890. The elaborate Italianate details, particularly the second story columns surrounding the four narrow windows, would have been very difficult to achieve with wood.

THIS IS A HOLDUP
On this site **Butch Cassidy** robbed his first bank at the age of 23. While working as a miner and ranch hand, he got to know the original building here, L.L. Nunn's San Miguel Valley Bank. On a sunny June morning in 1889 he and a gang of bandits entered the bank and ordered the assistant cashier to stick 'em up. They took all of the cash on hand – about $24,000 intended for miners' payroll – and fired a parting salute as they rode out of town. A posse pursued them, but the gang eluded them by using a series of fresh horses they had left at strategic points along their escape route. The bank later burned down.

MYSTERIOUS MURDER

Some folks said Jim Clark, who would later be Telluride's marshal, helped the Cassidy gang in the robbery. Some said he looked out for the little guys, but others said he was a crook who protected criminals. Clark got crosswise with Town Council and quit in April 1894. The following year, as he stepped out of the Brunswick Saloon, a bullet ripped through his chest. He staggered across the street into one of the nearby cribs and died. Rumors flew that the Town Council was behind it, but the shooter's identity and reasons for assassinating Clark remain a mystery.

19

Look diagonally across the intersection
of Colorado Avenue and Fir Street for your next clue.

This is the Tomkins Cristy Hardware Building.

EARLY HARDWARE

The business name painted on the side of this 1892 structure is Telluride's oldest example of a common practice on corner buildings in the late 1800s. The recessed corner entrance is flanked by three cast iron columns, similar to those on the Mahr Building.

The store was sold in 1896 to brothers H.H. and L.H. Tomkins, who owned hardware stores in Ouray, Durango, Leadville, Aspen, and Creede. Catering mostly to mining companies, the store, which became **Tomkins Cristy Hardware** in 1906, relied on the railroad to bring in merchandise and supplies. Except for the year after the 1893 silver crash, the 1890s proved to be a profitable decade for merchants in Telluride.

Butch Cassidy was known to have staked out the San Miguel Valley Bank from this building before his 1889 bank robbery.

HORSES MUST GO!

Business along Colorado Avenue was booming in 1899, enough so that some merchants petitioned the town to force the livery stables off the main thoroughfare. The *Telluride Journal* vehemently disagreed, arguing that it would be more appropriate to relegate "a dozen joints and dives" and "Chinese laundries and hop joints" to the back streets. The petitioners prevailed. **Rogers Livery** relocated from its home of 17 years to a new barn on a side street.

DANGEROUS WHEELS

By 1899, horses weren't the only conveyance that wore out their welcome on Colorado Avenue. The newspaper reported that bicycle riding on sidewalks had reached the point of "altogether too much scorching" along the main street. Several collisions had been narrowly averted, prompting the editor to predict someone would be "crippled or perhaps killed" unless the cyclists were banned.

20

Cross Fir Street and look
for this window on your right.

ROMANESQUE WONDER

This impressive 1892 structure was home to the **First National Bank** and L.L. Nunn's Telluride Electric Company offices. Nunn hired Denver architect James Murdoch and financed construction of the fortress-like Richardson Romanesque structure, using locally quarried sandstone and featuring arches flanking the corner entry, carved sandstone capitals over granite columns, stained glass windows, ornate wooden doors, and a three-story corner tower. The walk-in safe, which was moved from San Miguel Valley Bank – the one robbed by Butch Cassidy – after that building burned, can still be seen inside. The deteriorated tower had to be removed in 1940.

 This grand structure is another L.L. Nunn Building.

ELECTRIFYING SUCCESS

In 1898, **L.L. Nunn's** business in Telluride was at its peak. He was listed as a president of both the First National Bank and the Telluride Electrical Company, and a partner in both San Miguel Valley Bank and Keystone Gold Mining Company, which included the Gold King Mine. Along with partners, he also owned other business buildings in town. Ironically, Nunn was forced out of managing his power company in 1912 and devoted the remainder of his life to educating students about generating and transmitting electricity. The lifelong bachelor died in 1925 of tuberculosis.

MOVIE HOUSE

In 1925, First National Bank closed and the building was sold for $7,500. In 1935, it became the **Nugget Theater** and also housed the local Elks Lodge. The still-grand structure underwent a complete restoration in 2005. There are plans to restore the tower, which stood taller than the courthouse tower.

WOMEN DOCTORS

Two women doctors had offices in the First National Bank building. Dr. Eleanor Van Atta, sister of wealthy merchant and pack string owner William Beatty (W.B.) Van Atta, opened a medical practice here in 1890. She married Frank LeBlond, a salesman in her brother's store, and the couple moved to San Francisco.

Dr. Anna F.S. Brown came to Telluride around 1895 and practiced medicine here until 1923. "Dr. Brown's stork"

was frequently credited for delivering babies, and she cared for many female patients and children.

A WIDOW TOO YOUNG

Dr. Brown was married to Ira E. Brown, cashier for First National Bank. The two were frequent guests at important social events around town. Ira Brown and a partner invested in the Nellie Mine near Bear Creek, and only a few months later Ira was killed when he fell into the mine. After his death, Dr. Brown moved to an apartment in the bank and also opened her office in the building.

❝ I saw only my poverty, my loneliness and obscurity, but Doctor Brown ... in her divine femininity saw only my needs and the way to meet them.... She never ceased to come and cheer and comfort and encourage me ... She looked after my clothing and what was lacking she got and paid for out of her own purse ... Surely the kingdom of heaven is like unto Dr. Anna F.S. Brown."

– Isabell Inman
Telluride Journal, May 1908

Continue walking west on Colorado Avenue for one-half block.
Look across the street for your next clue.

This is the Pekkarine Building, which was named after a Finnish bootmaker.

TWO IN ONE

If you look closely, you can see that this commercial structure, known as the **Pekkarine Building,** was built in two phases. The roof of the east building

wraps up and over the west side, which therefore must have been built first. Both parts of the building were completed by 1893, several years before the family whose name it bears arrived in Telluride.

BOOTS MADE THE MAN

Aaro Pekkarine and his family emigrated from Finland and reached Telluride around the turn of the nineteenth century. Aaro was a well-regarded cobbler, or bootmaker, and had his shop in the basement. Eventually, they operated a general merchandise store on the main floor, and lived upstairs. Aaro's sister Aino came from Finland to help run her brother's business after his wife Anna died. Even though she was in her 60s, Aino attended first through fifth grade after she arrived so that she could learn English.

PARADE STAPLE

Townspeople recall that for many years, Aaro's son Eino drove the family's 1954 Nash in the Fourth of July parade, while his aunt, Aino, stood on top of the car dressed as the Statue of Liberty. Eino would stop the car periodically, get out, and play "The Star Spangled Banner" on his trumpet. They kept up this tradition into the 1960s.

CORNET CREEK FLOOD

On July 27, 1914, a massive cloudburst above Telluride opened and the valley was filled with a downpour. Emanating from high above Cornet Canyon, a torrent of water swooped through the Liberty Bell Mine waste dump and crashed down Cornet Creek. Trees and boulders were tossed down Oak Street and Colorado Avenue like sticks and marbles, leaving much of the town in ruins. Houses were ripped off foundations and businesses were buried. Terrified residents were barely able to escape the surging mass as **mud and debris** swamped the lower floors of businesses and residences along Columbia and Colorado avenues.

DARING RESCUE

Ermida Visintin was in her Oak Street home when the flood hit. Her husband arrived from his beer hall just in time for her to hand him their daughter through a window, and then escape herself. Vera Blakeley and her dog were less fortunate. She returned to her house to rescue her pet, and both perished – remarkably, the only victims in the deluge.

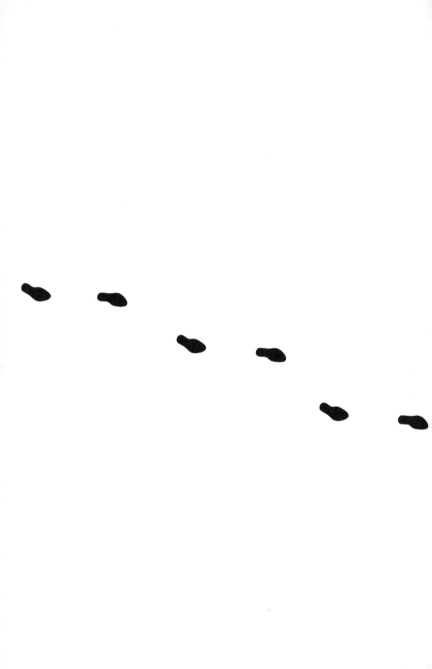

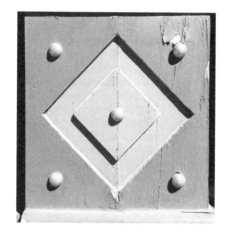

Continue walking west on Colorado Avenue until you see your next clue on a building to your right.

CROSS OF GOLD

The New Sheridan made history when William Jennings Bryan, long considered a great orator, delivered a variation of his famous Cross of Gold speech at the hotel in October 1902. First delivered when Bryan ran for president in 1896, the speech advocated basing the value of currency on both gold and silver – a cause that was near and dear to miners in the San Juans. But the cause had been lost long before he held forth in Telluride on that fall day in 1902.

 You are looking at the venerable Sheridan Block.

LAP OF LUXURY

These buildings have undergone many changes over the years. The two-story **Sheridan Hotel** was built on this corner in 1891, with calfskin-covered interior walls, a cherry bar imported from Austria and a saloon mirror from Paris. In 1897, the Sheridan Mine Company built the New Sheridan Hotel adjacent to it. Evidence of the third story, which was added in 1899, can be seen in the slightly different color of brick on the side. Higher quality brick was used for the front, and lesser quality for the sides – a common practice in Telluride.

The first Sheridan Hotel was destroyed by fire in December 1905, and almost 90 years later the current two-story replacement was carefully designed to resemble the original.

DESTRUCTIVE PATH

The sumptuously decorated Sheridan did not escape the **Cornet Creek Flood** of 1914 unscathed. From the San Miguel Courthouse to the First National Bank, a deep, pasty waste blanketed the town. Mud and debris flooded the Sheridan's ground floor, and filled the saloon with more than two feet of rubble.

23

Continue to the corner and walk past the small park,
then look for your next clue on your right.

You have found San Miguel County's second courthouse.

BETTER THAN THE FIRST

In 1883, San Miguel County was established and Telluride was named the county seat. The first courthouse, built across the street, burned a year after it was built. This impressive structure replaced it in 1887, built with local bricks on the sunnier, drier side of Colorado Avenue. Because this was designed as a civic building, there was a greater level of refinement in the details, in comparison to commercial buildings. For example, the **courthouse** has identical large, high-quality windows on all sides, unlike the New Sheridan Hotel. The bricks, however, are of lesser quality and have been painted throughout the years. The clock was installed in the tower during the 1976 Colorado centennial celebration.

In addition to its governmental use, the courthouse also served as a dance hall, meeting room, and a place for church services.

POLITICAL ACE

Harkening back to Telluride's early days when having the right touch with cards often determined a man's future, a tie vote in the 2001 Town Council election was decided by the luck of the draw. Standing on the courthouse steps, the town clerk held out a deck of cards to each of the candidates. **Stu Fraser** pulled the ace of spades and clinched the seat. He was elected mayor six years later.

HANG 'EM

The only **death sentence** issued from the court here was against Otis McDaniels, who was convicted of fatally shooting the Montezuma County Sheriff S.W. Dunlap near Placerville. McDaniels and his brother Herbert had robbed a Montezuma County rancher and left him to die. After they were captured in Glenwood Springs, Sheriff Dunlap and a deputy were bringing the two back for trial. The McDaniels brothers overpowered the lawmen, and Otis took the sheriff's gun and shot him. Otis was hanged on Valentine's Day 1936.

Walk just past the courthouse
and look through the fence to your right to find your next clue.

You have found the
Galloping Goose.

INGENUITY ON THE RAILS

After Telluride's mining declined in the 1920s, it became too costly to maintain the Rio Grande Southern's trains solely for passengers. In 1931, the railroad introduced the Galloping Goose to carry passengers, mail, and supplies across the San Juans. According to some locals, the Goose got its name from the riotous sight and sound the train made when its engine flaps were open. The first Goose was fabricated from the body of a Buick. Other Gooses were made from Winton or Pierce-Arrow automobile bodies and engines, and each car had flanged wheels adapted to run on the narrow gauge rail.

Locals and tourists alike used the Goose to travel into the mountains or to outlying towns like Ophir and Rico. The Galloping Goose served as transportation on the Rio Grande Southern from 1931 to 1949. Six original cars remain of this fleet, including Galloping Goose number four, which you see here.

> **"** I rode the Goose just for the fun of it. I remember I rode to Placerville one day. The front end and the back end were not fixed tightly. The front end would wave, and the back end would be going some other way. It stayed on the track, but the body parts would wiggle around. It was fun! It was quite a nice – in a way scenic – ride."
>
> – Wilma Lines

TAKING WING

At first, the **Galloping Goose** followed behind freight trains during winter storms to avoid snowslides or drifts that would stop it in its tracks. During the summer months, however, the Goose was free to fly along the rails alone. The Rio Grande Southern quickly attracted tourists wanting a scenic adventure. Although it was not substantial enough to save the railroad, it provided delighted passengers with memorable journeys through scenic places like Keystone Hill, Ophir Loop, and Trout Lake. The last Goose excursion in 1952 signalled the end of a unique chapter in railroading history.

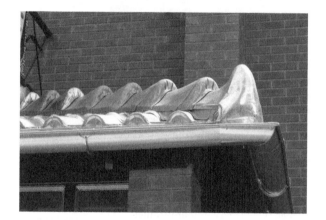

25

Walk back toward the Sheridan Hotel and turn left.
Watch for the clue as you walk uphill along the small park.

 You have found the Sheridan Opera House.

....

CURTAIN UP

In July 1913, the Segerberg Opera House was the last major building erected during Telluride's mining boom. Brothers J.A. and Aarid Segerberg promised to provide "the very best in the amusement way." Artists painted a Venetian scene on the olio curtain and stencilled floral designs throughout the interior. The brothers operated the 400-seat theater as the "Broadway of Telluride," featuring touring productions, high school and community musicals, concerts by their own orchestra, and galas until the Great Depression hit in 1929. The building eventually was renamed the **Sheridan Opera House** after the neighboring hotel and bar.

FESTIVE NEW LIFE

After the ski resort opened in 1972 and the economy shifted to tourism, Telluride began to reinvent itself into a town unlike any other destination in the country. To create this unique atmosphere, promoters organized many festivals, music, and performing arts events to operate year-round. In 1973, Bill and Stella Pence founded the now-famous Telluride Film Festival, using the Sheridan Opera House as its primary film venue. Other festivals, such as the Telluride Bluegrass Festival have established Telluride as an internationally recognized cultural and entertainment hub.

26

Continue walking north up Oak Street.
Turn and walk 1½ blocks west on Columbia Street.
Your clue will be on the right side of the street (north).

You have found where L.L. Nunn trained many of the first electrical engineering students in the nation.

WORK STUDY

In 1902, L.L. Nunn purchased this home for his new **Telluride Institute**, where Cornell University students could come to learn the practical application of electrical engineering.

In order to provide reliable, year-round power to the mines, someone had to be available around the clock every day, to do repairs if lightning or an avalanche damaged systems, interrupting power generation and transmission. To meet that need, Nunn created a work-study program. He recruited intelligent, intellectually curious men with an engineering background. They had to be young and have the stamina to work long hours at any of Nunn's generating stations. In addition to a small wage, they received invaluable hands-on training in the emerging field of electrical engineering. This house served as a residence and training institute for students. The Institute moved to Cornell in 1923, but this building is still referred to as the Cornell House.

NIAGARA POWER

After the Ames plant, Nunn built stations in other states. In 1897 he completed one in Provo Canyon, Utah. From 1902 to 1910, Lucien and his brother Paul designed and constructed one of the largest single hydroelectric stations in the world for the Ontario Power Company at Niagara Falls.

PINS ON A MAP

L.L. Nunn's electrical engineering students are often referred to as "**pin heads**." Though it sounds like a nickname for brainy students, the term was derived from Nunn's practice of sticking pins into a large map to keep track of the students' home towns.

Turn around and walk east on Columbia to Oak Street.
Your next clue photo will be on your left.

 You're in the neighborhood where Telluride's early titans of industry resided.

....

DAVIS HOUSE

E.L. Davis was a mining and real estate entrepreneur who became one of Telluride's wealthiest residents in the early 1900s. **His stately brick home** was completed in 1899 at a cost of $8,000. The house was built in the Classical Revival style, with columns and tooled stone sills, clearly reflecting the growing wealth of some Telluride residents. The Davises lived in Telluride for less than a decade, before Mr. Davis's health forced them to move to Salt Lake City in 1907.

In the 1920s, the house was purchased by Charles D. Waggoner, president of the Bank of Telluride. In 1929, Waggoner became involved in what became known as "The Great Waggoner Swindle."

FLU EPIDEMIC

The E.L. Davis house was temporarily converted to a hospital in the fall of 1918 when a worldwide epidemic reached Telluride. Influenza hit suddenly and severely the first week of October. State and local governments scrambled to control the outbreak with quarantines, bans on public meetings, and restrictions on travel. Even with businesses and schools closed in this small mountain town where pneumonia was already a familiar winter affliction, hundreds became ill.

The Telluride Miners Hospital quickly filled with patients. During the crisis, with miners being carried down from the mines each day, two saloons – including the Roma Saloon on Colorado Avenue – were converted into makeshift hospitals, as was the Davis house.

> **❝** [In 1918] I had a young brother who was only nine months old. He was such a fat and healthy little boy. Then Mother got the flu and gave it to him – he died quickly. Mother's health was pretty bad, so she didn't get to go to the funeral. Daddy and I went to the **[Lone Tree] cemetery**. It was a horse-drawn hearse, and I can remember when we went down the streets of Telluride to the caemetery. People would only peek out the windows from their curtains or shades when they saw the hearse go by. I said to Daddy, 'Why do they peek and then slam the curtain down?' And he said, 'They think that someone in their family will be next.' I can remember that 'cause he had tears in his eyes. It was his only son at that time, and it was so sad."
>
> – Nina Price

A NEVER-ENDING BATTLE

Dr. Anna F.S. Brown was Telluride's public health officer when the influenza epidemic hit. Infectious diseases were not a new concern for Dr. Brown. As public health officer off and on since 1901, she had pushed for accurate diagnosis and quarantine of patients with diphtheria, cholera, small pox, and scarlet fever, sometimes in conflict with other doctors. People with contagious diseases were supposed to be confined to their homes or the "pest house" on the outskirts of town. When she learned that milk deliverymen were taking used bottles from one customer and filling them for the next, she campaigned for sterilization of all bottles. She also fought to have mining company outhouses removed from the banks of Cornet Creek, which was the source of Telluride's water.

| 81

28

Continue east on Columbia, crossing Oak and Fir streets. Your next clue photo will be on your left at the corner of Fir Street and Columbia.

 You have found Telluride's first center of learning.

SCHOOL DAYS

By 1897, teachers in Telluride earned about $60 a month. With immigrants from many countries seeking a new life in the prosperous American West, Telluride became a multilingual town. Many **school children** in these immigrant families did not speak English initially, but quickly learned and helped their parents and siblings to master the language as well.

TELLURIDE TOWN HALL

One of Telluride's oldest surviving buildings, this structure was built as a school in 1883. In 1895, with an enrollment of more than 190 students, a new school was built farther west on Columbia Avenue. In 1896, the old school was converted into the **town hall** and also used by the town's volunteer fire department.

❝When I started school in 1910, I couldn't speak English at all. I lived on West Pacific with all the other Finn families. When anybody came over from Finland to Telluride, they found a room with a Finnish boarding house or Finnish family.... Mother would only [speak] Finn. She even went to night school for a while. I used to help her to read English."

– William Ranta

FIRE DRILL

The Fire Department is Telluride's oldest established organization. An efficient fire department was essential because mining camps, mills, and early settlements were built primarily of wood. A small blaze in one frame building could easily spread to the entire block. The earliest firefighting method consisted of bucket brigades. Later, a wagon carried a water tank, which was pulled by men and eventually drawn by horses. In 1886, Telluride had eight fire hydrants. By 1904, there were thirty-eight.

Throughout the year, teams of volunteer fireman trained long hours **carrying and pulling water hoses** down Colorado Avenue so they would be able to respond to fires quickly. Along with their other fire-fighting duties, the department sponsored Telluride's annual Fourth of July celebrations, including regional tug-of-war and hose-team races with neighboring mining towns, such as Ouray and Silverton.

"I remember when the Smuggler Mill burnt down. That was on the 20th of June 1920, and the whistles blew in town.... The horses were ready in the stall, and the harnesses were above the horses, so that all the firemen had to do was drop the harnesses and buckle them up. The fire wagon was right behind it... . Well, the one that was on [duty] that night was [Lee] Long. When he hooked up the team, he didn't hook up one rein to the bridle. He couldn't turn them down Main Street, and couldn't turn 'em out toward the mills. So they came straight down Fir Street. When the wagon came, it hit [a boxcar] so hard that it threw the driver [Long] clear out on the street. Killed him right there. I heard it from right here in our living room.... [mine owner] Bulkeley Wells decided after that fire to buy Telluride a [gas] fire wagon."

– Walter "Shorty" Larson

☞ Before continuing, look north up Fir Street,
you will see a red sandstone building, which was once the
town's hospital. You will learn more about this building,
now the Telluride Historical Museum,
when you finish your tour there.

29

Continue east on Columbia past Town Hall and Rebekah Hall
on your left. Your next clue will be on your left
before you get to Pine Street.

| 87

 You've found a focal point of past labor strife.

·······································

MINERS UNION HOSPITAL

Most miners worked ten- to twelve-hour shifts, seven days a week in dangerous conditions. Death and injury were common, often grisly. Men fell down shafts, became ensnared in equipment, or were crushed in cave-ins. The threat of fires and avalanches was constant. Resentment against wealthy mine owners intensified. By 1896, many Telluride miners had joined the militant Western Federation of Miners (WFM) to demand improved working conditions and pay. The WFM built this ornate brick hospital in 1902 for union miners, to spite the mine owners as much as to care for the sick.

> ❝ During the time of the strike in Telluride, there were a lot of men sitting around the boarding house [my mother] owned, not doing anything or paying their bills. So she [told] the manager of the Tomboy Mine . . . to get these men back to work so they could pay their board bills. . . They were hiring "scabs" instead of the local people. Afterwards, they started hiring local men at the mines again."
>
> – William Rautio

GUARD SUMMONED

On September 1, 1903, mill workers went on strike to reduce their workday from twelve hours to eight. By October 31, the strike spread to the mines. The National Guard was summoned, and, in 1904, martial law was declared for several months, forcing many of the union leaders out of town. The Guard took over Hall's Hospital and denied care to union miners. Mine owners' money and the governor's power prevailed, breaking strikes across Colorado in 1905. Miners and mill workers went back to work for the same low wages, in the same appalling conditions. The Miners Union Hospital soon was converted to other uses.

Turn left (north) on Pine Street and walk one block.
Stop at the street corner and look down the street for your next clue.

 You have found St. Patrick's Church.

....

RESTORED CHURCH

St. Patrick's Church is the only historic Telluride church that remains active today. The Gothic Revival building, with its steeply pitched roof, arched windows, and exposed interior rafters, was built in 1896 for $4,800. Many of the Catholic families from Austria and Italy attended the church and this part of town quickly became known as Catholic Hill.

By the mid-1930s, in the throes of the Great Depression, Telluride's population dropped below 500. Even the priests left town, and people had to attend services in Montrose, nearly 100 miles away. St. Patrick's Church, still in its original location, was lovingly restored in the 1990s. If you have time after the tour, visit the inside of the church and notice the carved wooden figures, the church's original Stations of the Cross, on the walls.

> **"** People nowadays have no idea how really rough that **Depression** was. Nobody had any money. We barely had enough to eat. . . . Married couples got $15 a month for groceries, and single people got $5. If you had no other income, that was it! Around 1930, the county hired a bunch of us – gave us a week's work, I think, in the wintertime just shoveling snow. We also tried to raise a garden. In this high altitude, about all you could raise was potatoes and carrots. . . . A lot of places it was probably worse. In a little town like this, it didn't seem so bad."
>
> – Allene and Water Pera

31

Turn left (west) on Galena Avenue and walk one block to Fir Street. Turn right (north) and continue one block to find your clue.

This grand stone building was once a hospital. It's now the Telluride Museum.

HOSPITAL LINEAGE

This building is one of the crowning glories of Telluride's National Historic Landmark District. Constructed in 1896 by **Dr. H.C. Hall** using distinctive red sandstone from a local quarry. The hospital was known as Hall's Hospital, Hadley Hospital (for another doctor), American Legion Hospital, and simply, Community Hospital. In 1900, visiting the doctor at the hospital cost $1 and home visits ranged from $2 to $5. This was quite expensive, considering the average mine worker's pay and boarding costs.

Before the Miners Union Hospital was built, injured or sick miners and their families were cared for here. Tragically, men with severe silicosis, commonly known as miners' consumption, rarely left alive.

FIRST BORN

In addition to treating injured and sick miners, the hospital also served business people and the growing number of women and children in Telluride. **Harriet Fish Backus**, author of *The Tomboy Bride,* gave birth to the first baby born in the hospital in 1901. You can learn more about her life inside the museum.

> " Across the driveway, a large cellar was built into the hillside [with] ample storage for fruits, vegetables, and perishables.... a short distance away was a big wooden ice cream freezer. Every Sunday the cook's helpers would churn the homemade ice cream for doctors, nurses, and even patients. Every Sunday a different flavor: strawberry, cherry, raspberry, and pineapple."
>
> – Alma Mary Clifton whose Aunt Isabella was in charge of the hospital kitchen

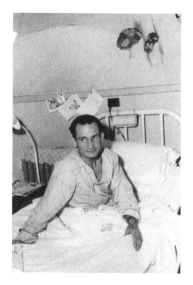

BRAVE DOCTOR

In July 1949, **Dr. George C. Balderston** garnered national attention when he removed his own appendix at the Telluride Hospital. Nurses, including Arlene Reid, were present to assist, as was another doctor who administered a spinal anesthetic. Balderston performed the operation while seated, and closed the incision himself, all within 45 minutes. Dr. Balderston explained that he wanted to experience the effects of local anesthesia and determine how quickly surgical patients could get "back on their feet." He returned to work two days later. You can learn more about Balderston inside the museum.

FROM HOSPITAL TO MUSEUM

More than 600 babies were born at the hospital and thousands of miners and their families were treated. Dr. Joe Parker, Telluride's sole physician in the 1930s, earned $25 a month as city health officer and $25 a month as San Miguel County health officer. He and his wife, a registered nurse, also earned $235 a month for providing basic family health care to the town residents.

In 1934, the American Legion bought the hospital at a county auction and furnished it with new equipment. Although the hospital faced monthly deficits and threats of closure, Dr. Parker kept it running safely. During his fifteen years in Telluride, he served as mayor, school board president, county coroner, deputy sheriff, and volunteer fireman.

Years after the hospital closed in 1964, one of the nurses, Arlene Reid, reopened it as the San Miguel Historical Society, and became the first museum director. People fondly recall Arlene's outgoing personality. In 1994, the building again faced possible destruction when it was condemned. Instead, Telluride voters approved a bond and tax to support it. The building was fully restored and reopened in December 2005.

Great Finish!

We hope you have enjoyed learning about Telluride and the people who have called it home over the past century and a half. Perhaps you can envision those early prospectors hacking away at the mountains in search of gold, the first merchants building and stocking their stores, or the packers whose mules and horses kept goods and ore moving.

> ☞ **To return to Colorado Avenue,**
> **walk south down Fir Street to Pacific Avenue.**
> **Turning right, or west, will take you back toward**
> **our starting point at the old train depot.**

If you've enjoyed learning about Telluride's colorful history, and want to know more.

Visit Lone Tree Cemetery at the east end of Colorado Avenue

Explore the courthouse (stop 23)

Attend a concert at the Sheridan Opera House (stop 25)

Ride the free gondola up to Mountain Village - Oak Street Plaza

Stop at the Telluride Visitors Center - 630 W. Colorado Ave.

TO LEARN MORE

Telluride: From Pick to Powder, by Richard L. and Suzanne Fetter

Conversations at 9000 Feet, by Davine Pera

The R.G.S. Story: Rio Grande Southern - Volume II: Telluride, Pandora, and the Mines Above, by Russ Collman

The Corpse on Boomerang Road, by MaryJoy Martin

Notorious Telluride, by Carol Turner

ACKNOWLEDGMENTS

A sincere thank you to the following individuals for their inspiration and encouragement in the creation of this book: the board members of the Telluride Historical Museum, especially Todd Brown and Rudy Davison for their years of research into the people and places of Telluride; Anne Gerhard and Lucas Fredericks for their editing and research assistance; Jeanne Brako and Esther Greenfield at the Center of Southwest Studies; the Denver Public Library, the Wilkinson Public Library, and the Lone Tree Cemetery; and Bob Mather and Lauren Bloemsma with the Town of Telluride.

We would also like to give a sincere thank you to the Durango Herald Small Press and Elizabeth Green, without whom this book would not be possible. Their oversight and guidance throughout writing and editing made the entire process a wonderful learning experience for everyone at the Telluride Historical Museum. Thank you!

Erica Kinias was born in Durango and grew up under the southwestern skies of Tucson, Arizona. After receiving her bachelor's degree in history at Arizona State University, Erica lived in Bellingham, Washington, and then in London, England, where she received her master's degree in museum studies from the University of London's Institute of Archaeology. She served as curator at Chiddingstone Castle, Kent, before returning to the Southwest to work as grants manager with the Arizona Humanities Council, helping museums and libraries plan and fund humanities-based projects. Erica joined the Telluride Historical Museum as executive director in 2012, and has loved exploring the region's awe-inspiring landscape and history.

PHOTO CREDITS

All photographs are the property of Telluride Historical Museum except:

Page 8, Otto Mears, San Juan County Historical Society

Page 90, St. Patrick's Church, Denver Public Library Western History collection

INDEX

CPSIA information can be obtained
at www.ICGtesting.com
Printed in the USA
FSOW03n0028120615
7868FS